This Christmas Memory Book belongs to

....

Ellie Claire® Gift & Paper Corp.
Brentwood, TN 37027
EllieClaire.com
A Worthy Publishing Company

Christmas Memory Book
Remembering Special Moments
© 2013 Ellie Claire Gift & Paper Corp.

ISBN 978-1-60936-813-5

Scripture quotations taken from The Holy Bible, New International Version® (NIV)®. Copyright © 1973, 1978, 1984, 2011 by Biblica.Used by permission of Zondervan. All rights reserved worldwide. The New American Standard Bible® (NASB), Copyright © 1960, 1962, 1963, 1968, 1971, 1972, 1973, 1975, 1977, 1995 by The Lockman Foundation. Used by permission. The Holy Bible, King James Version (KJV). The Holy Bible, New King James Version (NKJV). Copyright © 1997, 1990, 1985, 1983 by Thomas Nelson, Inc. All rights reserved.

Stock or custom editions of Ellie Claire titles may be purchased in bulk for educational, business, ministry, fundraising, or sales promotional use. For information, please email info @EllieClaire.com.

Compiled by Jill Olson
Cover design by David Carlson | studiogearbox.com
Interior design and typesetting by Jeff Jansen | aestheticoup.net

Printed in China

1 2 3 4 5 6 7 8 9 – 18 17 16 15 14 13

Christmas Celebration

Let cedar fill the air

With its spicy sweetness rare

Wake the carol—sound the chime—

Welcome! Merry Christmas time!

HELEN CHASE

Special Guests—

Memorable Gatherings—

'Tis Christmas morning: Christmas mirth
And joyous voices fill the house.

THOMAS BAILEY ALDRICH

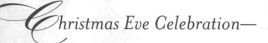

Christmas Eve Celebration—

Christmas Day Celebration—

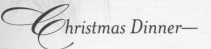Christmas Dinner—

Christmas Traditions Observed—

Thoughtful Gestures and Cherished Gifts—

For somehow, not only at Christmas,

but all the long year through,

the joy that you give to others

is the joy that comes back to you.

JOHN GREENLEAF WHITTIER

Holiday Photo

{Adhere a favorite Christmas photo here}

Behold, I bring you good news of great joy
which will be for all the people.

LUKE 2:10 NASB

Christmas Greeting Sent

{Adhere Christmas card or newsletter here}

Special Events—

Rejoice in the Lord always. I will say it again: Rejoice!

PHILIPPIANS 4:4 NIV

The Best, Funniest, Most Challenging, Touching, Embarrassing, or Amazing Memories of this Christmas—

Reflections from the Season—

The coming of Jesus at Bethlehem

brought joy to the world and to every human heart.

May His coming this Christmas

bring to each one of us that peace

and joy that He desires to give.

MOTHER TERESA

Christmas Celebration

....

Christmas Year

It is Christmas in the heart

that puts Christmas in the air.

W. T. ELLIS

*Special Guests—*

Memorable Gatherings—

Does not the Scripture say that the Christ will come from David's family and from Bethlehem, the town where David lived?

JOHN 7:42 NIV

Christmas Eve Celebration—

Christmas Day Celebration—

Christmas Dinner—

Christmas Traditions Observed—

Thoughtful Gestures and Cherished Gifts—

I love the Christmas-tide, and yet

I notice this, each year I live;

I always like the gifts I get,

But how I love the gifts I give!

CAROLYN WELLS

Holiday Photo

{Adhere a favorite Christmas photo here}

I will give You thanks with all my heart.

PSALM 138:1 NASB

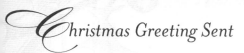

Christmas Greeting Sent

{Adhere Christmas card or newsletter here}

Special Events—

Let his joy come to our weary world through us.

GERALD KENNEDY

*The Best, Funniest, Most Challenging, Touching, Embarrassing,
or Amazing Memories of this Christmas—*

Reflections from the Season—

What if Christmas day were both a beginning and an end?

The beginning of a celebration of Jesus

that would not end until the next Christmas,

when it would begin all over again?

MICHAEL CARD

Christmas Celebration

....

Christmas Year

Christmas, my child, is love in action.

DALE EVANS ROGERS

Special Guests—

Memorable Gatherings—

Suddenly there was with the angel a multitude of the heavenly host praising God, and saying, Glory to God in the highest, and on earth peace, good will toward men.

LUKE 2:13–14 KJV

Christmas Eve Celebration—

Christmas Day Celebration—

Christmas Dinner—

Christmas Traditions Observed—

Thoughtful Gestures and Cherished Gifts—

The joy of brightening each other's lives...

With generous gifts

Becomes for us the magic of Christmas.

W. C. JONES

Holiday Photo

{Adhere a favorite Christmas photo here}

Bless the LORD, O my soul, and all that is within me, *bless* His holy name.

PSALM 103:1 NASB

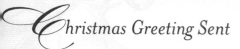

Christmas Greeting Sent

{Adhere Christmas card or newsletter here}

Special Events—

Had my house been filled at Bethlehem,
What should I have done...
Would I have guessed
The Prince of Peace was come?

ALLISON C. WOOD

The Best, Funniest, Most Challenging, Touching, Embarrassing, or Amazing Memories of this Christmas—

Reflections from the Season—

I heard the bells on Christmas day

Their old familiar carols play,

And wild and sweet the words repeat

Of peace on earth, good will to men.

HENRY WADSWORTH LONGFELLOW

Christmas Celebration

Christmas Year

An angel announced His conception and gave Him His name.

The heavenly host sang a glorious anthem at His birth.

By the extraordinary star, the very heavens indicated His coming.

BILLY GRAHAM

Special Guests—

Memorable Gatherings—

When they saw the star, they rejoiced exceedingly with great joy.

MATTHEW 2:10 NASB

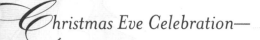

Christmas Eve Celebration—

Christmas Day Celebration—

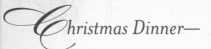*Christmas Dinner—*

Christmas Traditions Observed—

Thoughtful Gestures and Cherished Gifts—

The holidays are welcome to me

partly because they are such rallying

points for the affections which get

so much thrust aside in the business

and preoccupations of daily life.

GEORGE E. WOODBERRY

Holiday Photo

{Adhere a favorite Christmas photo here}

O holy night, the stars are brightly shining
It is the night of our dear Savior's birth.

PLACIDE CAPPEAU

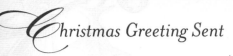

Christmas Greeting Sent

{Adhere Christmas card or newsletter here}

 *Special Events—*

Like God, Christmas is timeless
and eternal, from everlasting to
everlasting. It is something even more
than what happened that night in
starlit little Bethlehem; it has been
behind the stars forever. There was
Christmas in the heart of God
before the world was formed.

ROY ROGERS

The Best, Funniest, Most Challenging, Touching, Embarrassing, or Amazing Memories of this Christmas—

Reflections from the Season—

Scanning the heavens I am reminded

of another star from long ago.

GALILEO GALILEI

Christmas Celebration

....

Christmas Year

Behold, the virgin shall be with child and shall bear a Son,

and they shall call His name Immanuel,"

which translated means "God with us."

MATTHEW 1:23 NASB

Special Guests—

Memorable Gatherings—

Christmas is a time of the heart, not just a date. Its meaning transcends time.

Christmas Eve Celebration—

Christmas Day Celebration—

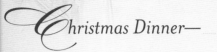 *Christmas Dinner—*

Christmas Traditions Observed—

Thoughtful Gestures and Cherished Gifts—

I will honor Christmas in my heart,

and try to keep it all the year.

CHARLES DICKENS

Holiday Photo

{Adhere a favorite Christmas photo here}

She brought forth her firstborn son, and wrapped him in swaddling clothes,
and laid him in a manger.

LUKE 2:7 KJV

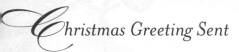

Christmas Greeting Sent

{Adhere Christmas card or newsletter here}

Special Events—

Good news from heaven the angels bring;
glad tidings to the earth they sing:
To us this day a child is given,
To crown us with the joy of heaven.

MARTIN LUTHER

The Best, Funniest, Most Challenging, Touching, Embarrassing,
or Amazing Memories of this Christmas—

Reflections from the Season—

Angels we have heard on high

Sweetly singing o'er the plain,

And the mountains in reply

Echoing the joyous strain.

Christmas Celebration

....

Christmas Year

At Christmas play and make good cheer,

for Christmas comes but once a year.

Thomas Tusser

Special Guests—

Memorable Gatherings—

A cheerful heart is good medicine.

PROVERBS 17:22 NIV

Christmas Eve Celebration—

Christmas Day Celebration—

Christmas Dinner—

Christmas Traditions Observed—

Thoughtful Gestures and Cherished Gifts—

The heart of the giver

makes the gift

dear and precious.

MARTIN LUTHER

Holiday Photo

{Adhere a favorite Christmas photo here}

There has been only one Christmas—the rest are anniversaries.

W. J. CAMERON

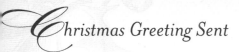

Christmas Greeting Sent

{Adhere Christmas card or newsletter here}

 _Special Events—_

Many merry Christmases, many happy New Years. Unbroken friendships,
great accumulations of cheerful recollections and affections on earth, and heaven for us all.

CHARLES DICKENS

The Best, Funniest, Most Challenging, Touching, Embarrassing, or Amazing Memories of this Christmas—

Reflections from the Season—

Forth to the wood did merry men go,

to gather in the mistletoe.

SIR WALTER SCOTT

Christmas Celebration

Christmas Year

The things we do at Christmas are touched with a certain

extravagance, as beautiful, in some of its aspects,

as the extravagance of nature in June.

ROBERT COLLYER

Special Guests—

Memorable Gatherings—

Love came down at Christmas / Love all lovely, love divine;
Love was born at Christmas / Star and angels gave the sign.

CHRISTINA ROSSETTI

Christmas Eve Celebration—

Christmas Day Celebration—

Christmas Dinner—

Christmas Traditions Observed—

Thoughtful Gestures and Cherished Gifts—

To be grateful is to recognize the love

of God in everything He has given us—

and He has given us everything.

Every breath we draw is a gift of His love,

every moment of existence is a gift of grace.

THOMAS MERTON

Holiday Photo

{Adhere a favorite Christmas photo here}

You are a...people for God's own possession,
so that you may proclaim the excellencies of Him who has called you.

1 PETER 2:9 NASB

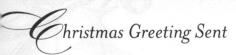

Christmas Greeting Sent

{Adhere Christmas card or newsletter here}

 _Special Events—_

What keeps the wild hope of
Christmas alive year after year...
is the haunting dream that
the child who was born that day
may yet be born again even
in us and our own snowbound,
snowblind longing for Him.

FREDERICK BUECHNER

The Best, Funniest, Most Challenging, Touching, Embarrassing, or Amazing Memories of this Christmas—

Reflections from the Season—

Then let us all with one accord

Sing praises to our heavenly Lord...

Noel, Noel, Noel, Noel

Born is the King of Israel!

Christmas Celebration

Christmas Year

Our hearts grow tender with childhood memories and love

of kindred, and we are better throughout the year for having,

in spirit, become a child again at Christmas-time.

LAURA INGALLS WILDER

Special Guests—

Memorable Gatherings—

Every hearth is aflame, and the beautiful sing
In the homes of the nations that Jesus is King!

JOSIAH GILBERT HOLLAND

Christmas Eve Celebration—

Christmas Day Celebration—

Christmas Dinner—

Christmas Traditions Observed—

Thoughtful Gestures and Cherished Gifts—

The generous will

themselves be blessed.

PROVERBS 22:9 NIV

Holiday Photo

{Adhere a favorite Christmas photo here}

Beloved, let us love one another, for love is of God;

and everyone who loves is born of God and knows God.

I JOHN 4:7 NKJV

Christmas Greeting Sent

{Adhere Christmas card or newsletter here}

Special Events—

The most vivid memories of
Christmases past are usually not
of gifts given or received, but of the
spirit of love, the special warmth
of Christmas worship, the cherished
little habits of the home, the results
of others acting in the spirit of Christ.

LOIS RAND

The Best, Funniest, Most Challenging, Touching, Embarrassing, or Amazing Memories of this Christmas—

Reflections from the Season—

Hark! the herald angels sing

Glory to the newborn King;

Peace on earth and mercy mild,

God and sinners reconciled.

Christmas Celebration

....

Christmas is the season for kindling the

fire of hospitality in the hall,

the genial flame of charity in the heart.

WASHINGTON IRVING

*S*pecial Guests—

*M*emorable Gatherings—

The shepherds returned, glorifying and praising God
for all the things they had heard and seen.

LUKE 2:20 NIV

Christmas Eve Celebration—

_____

_____

_____

_____

_____

Christmas Day Celebration—

_____

_____

_____

_____

_____

Christmas Dinner—

Christmas Traditions Observed—

Thoughtful Gestures and Cherished Gifts—

I believe the most important Christmas gifts

are not those under the tree—

the best gifts are the love of family and friends,

the joy of relationship with God.

Holiday Photo

{Adhere a favorite Christmas photo here}

I greet you; not quite as the world sends greetings, but with profound esteem,
and with the prayer that for you, now and forever, the day breaks and the shadows flee away.

Frà Giovanni Giocondo

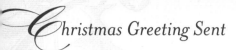

Christmas Greeting Sent

{Adhere Christmas card or newsletter here}

Special Events—

*The simple shepherds
heard the voice of an
angel and found their
Lamb; the wise men
saw the light of a star
and found their Wisdom.*

FULTON J. SHEEN

The Best, Funniest, Most Challenging, Touching, Embarrassing,
or Amazing Memories of this Christmas—

Reflections from the Season—

Along the hills of Galilee

the white flocks sleeping lay

When Christ, the child of Nazareth,

was born on Christmas day.

DINAH MARIA MULOCK CRAIK

Christmas Celebration

....

Christmas Year

Where charity stands watching

and faith holds wide the door,

the dark night wakes—the glory breaks,

Christmas comes once more.

PHILLIPS BROOKS

Special Guests—

Memorable Gatherings—

Blessed are those who dwell in your house;
they are ever praising you.

PSALM 84:4 NIV

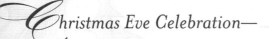

Christmas Eve Celebration—

Christmas Day Celebration—

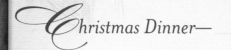

Christmas Dinner—

Christmas Traditions Observed—

Thoughtful Gestures and Cherished Gifts—

The coming of the babe in the manger was

not the first time Christ entered this world—

He has always been there with the Father—

and the story of His love reaching out to man

began as long ago as time itself.

GLORIA GAITHER

Holiday Photo

{Adhere a favorite Christmas photo here}

Mary said: "My soul glorifies the Lord and my spirit rejoices in God."

LUKE 1:47 NIV

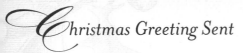

Christmas Greeting Sent

{Adhere Christmas card or newsletter here}

Special Events—

All the great purposes of God
culminate in Him. The greatest
and most momentous fact which
the history of the world records
is the fact of His birth.

CHARLES H. SPURGEON

The Best, Funniest, Most Challenging, Touching, Embarrassing, or Amazing Memories of this Christmas—

Reflections from the Season—

*Gratitude is a twofold love — love coming to visit us
and love running out to greet a welcome guest.*

HENRY VAN DYKE